W9-CRH-660

The Story of Guns

How They Changed the World

The World Transformed

— ◻ BY KATHERINE MCLEAN BREVARD

Content Adviser:
David Kennedy, former curator, Cody Firearms Museum, Cody, Wyoming,
and author of *Guns of the Wild West*

Reading Adviser:
Alexa L. Sandmann, Ed.D., Professor of Literacy,
College and Graduate School of Education, Health, and
Human Services, Kent State University

Compass Point Books
151 Good Counsel Drive
P.O. Box 669
Mankato, MN 56002-0669

Printed in the United States of America in North Mankato, Minnesota.
092009
005618CGS10

Editor: Jennifer Fretland VanVoorst
Designer: Ashlee Suker
Media Researcher: Eric Gohl
Library Consultant: Kathleen Baxter
Production Specialist: Jane Klenk

Image Credits: Alamy/Interfoto, 13; Alamy/Jim West, 55; Alamy/Mary Evans
Picture Library, 5; Alamy/North Wind Picture Archives, 19, 20, 26; Alamy/
RIA Novosti, 44; Alamy/The London Art Archive, 8; AP Images/FBI, 31; AP
Images/Mike Derer, 57; Art Resource, N.Y./Erich Lessing, 7; Courtesy of Army
Art Collection, U.S. Army Center of Military History, 21, 22; Getty Images Inc./
AFP, 47; Getty Images Inc./AFP/Andreas Solaro, 51; Getty Images Inc./AFP/
Zoom Dosso, 49; Getty Images Inc./Dorling Kindersley/Geoff Brightling, 29;
Getty Images Inc./Hulton Archive, 12; Getty Images Inc./MPI, 23; Getty Images
Inc./Popperfoto, 11, 37; Getty Images Inc./Science & Society Picture Library, 17,
36; Getty Images Inc./Scott Barbour, 1, cover; Getty Images Inc./Stock Montage,
24; Getty Images Inc./Three Lions, 35; Getty Images Inc./Tim Boyle, 54; Getty
Images Inc./Time Life Pictures/Joseph Louw, 53; Library of Congress, 27, 38,
39, 41; Shutterstock/Victorian Traditions, 15; The Bridgeman Art Library/Peter
Newark Pictures/Private Collection, 42; The Bridgeman Art Library/Private
Collection, 33;The Granger Collection, New York, 6; Wikipedia, public-domain
image, 45.

Library of Congress Cataloging-in-Publication Data
Brevard, Katherine McLean.
  The story of guns: how they changed the world / by Katherine
McLean Brevard.
    p. cm. — (The world transformed) Includes bibliographical
references and index.
  ISBN 978-0-7565-4313-6 (library binding)
  1. Firearms—Juvenile literature. I. Title. II. Series.
TS533.M455 2010
303.48'3—dc22   2009034857

Visit Compass Point Books on the Internet at *www.compasspointbooks.com*
or e-mail your request to *custserv@compasspointbooks.com*

Table of Contents

Chapter 1

From "Fire Medicine" to Firepower

For hundreds of thousands of years, people have tried to find ways to launch deadly objects at animals and humans. They threw rocks and later hurled stones in slings and in catapults. They sharpened sticks and made them into spears. Eventually they made smaller, lighter shafts called arrows and used them to hunt animals for food. They also used them to kill people they felt threatened by.

In many ways, though, the story of guns begins with the story of gunpowder. It probably was invented in China and was developed gradually over centuries. Gunpowder is made of saltpeter, sulfur, and charcoal. By the first century, saltpeter and sulfur were widely used in Chinese medicines. Gunpowder was probably invented by a group of Taoist monks who were trying to create something that would let people live forever. Many Chinese thought powders thrown into the air and on people and objects had magical properties, and Emperor Wu Di of the Han dynasty (206 B.C.E.–220 C.E.) paid for the monks' research. In 142 C.E., a monk named

Wei Boyang wrote *Book of the Kinship of the Three*, in which he detailed the experiments. The monks had not found the secret of eternal life, but the book describes a mixture of three mineral powders that would violently "fly and dance." The monks had combined sulfur and saltpeter with charcoal to create a substance they called *huo yao* ("fire medicine"). Before it was used to make fireworks and to propel lethal objects, huo yao—gunpowder—was used to treat skin diseases and kill insects.

Around 700 C.E., T'ang dynasty emperors began to use this seemingly magical substance to host great fireworks

Early Chinese emperors used fireworks to entertain guests and frighten intruders.

displays that lasted for hours. By 850 Chinese inventors had learned that they could make weapons using gunpowder, including flamethrowers, bombs, and mines. First the army used gunpowder in rockets. Later soldiers put small stone cannonballs inside bamboo tubes and shot the cannonballs out by lighting gunpowder at one end. This is basically the same way guns and cannons work today.

The direct ancestors of guns were called fire lances. They were gunpowder-filled, funnel-shaped tubes attached to the end of spears and used as flame-throwers. Rocks and pieces of jagged metal were often placed in the barrels with the gunpowder so they would shoot out with the flames. Larger versions of fire lances had a bamboo or wooden pole to prop up the front of the weapon to help aim it.

Eventually gunpowder was made more explosive, which made fire lances

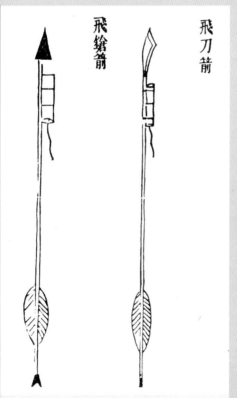

飛鎗箭　飛刀箭

The Chinese used gunpowder to propel arrows in the 11th century.

even more powerful. Metal replaced the paper and bamboo that fire lance barrels had been made from. Shrapnel was replaced by metal balls that filled the barrel more fully. The refined design included the three basic features of a gun: It has a metal barrel. It uses high-nitrate gunpowder as a propellant. And the projectile it fires almost completely fills the muzzle so the gunpowder explosion produces maximum force.

An illustration from *Bellifortis*, a 15th century manual of military technology, shows a soldier shooting a fire lance.

The Story of Guns

The earliest depiction of a gun that archaeologists have found is a sculpture from a cave in China that dates to the 1100s. The sculpture shows a man firing a long gun with a vase-shaped barrel. Flames and a ball are erupting from the end of the barrel.

The Chinese did not stop making larger guns, however. Mongol conqueror Genghis Khan used cannons in his wars. The Chinese returned fire with cannons that they called "heaven-shaking thunder." And Genghis Khan's grandson Kublai Khan used them during the successful siege of the Chinese city of Siang Yang from 1268 to 1273. The victory is celebrated in traditional Chinese songs as "the days and nights when the sound of explosions shook the sky." The oldest surviving gun, made of bronze, was discovered

Genghis Khan was a fierce warrior who founded the largest land empire in history.

at a site where Chinese foot soldiers, armed with guns, suppressed the rebellion of a Mongol prince in 1288.

Chinese emperors tried to keep guns a secret, but by the 12th century their secret had gotten out, and people in the Islamic Empire and later the Roman Empire learned to use gunpowder to power deadly new weapons. After that it wasn't long before people throughout Europe found out how to use the substance they called "Chinese salt" and learned how to make guns.

Gunpowder in Europe

By the 13th century, references to gunpowder began to show up in European writings. In about 1257, English scientist Roger Bacon wrote, "We can, with saltpeter and other substances, compose artificially a fire that can be launched over long distances." He later wrote about "a child's toy of sound and fire and explosion made in various parts of the world with powder of saltpeter, sulfur and charcoal of hazelwood." Marcus Graecus' *Liber Ignium* (*Book of Fires*)—a collection of formulas from about 1300—includes some gunpowder recipes, including one for "flying fire" and another for "artificial thunder."

Chapter 2

Guns Go Portable

No one is quite sure how people in Europe learned about guns. One theory is that guns and gunpowder made their way along the Silk Road, a trading route through Central Asia. Another is that they were brought to Europe during the Mongol invasion in the first half of the 13th century. A third theory is that the famous Venetian trader and traveler Marco Polo brought them to Italy when he returned from China in 1295.

Regardless of how they arrived, by the mid-13th century people in Italy and France had invented cannons and used them to shoot large, heavy iron balls at their enemies. The first cannons were inaccurate. They were used at close range and only against big targets—often the walls of a castle or the buildings of a town. In 1453 Turkish invaders used cannons to knock down the city walls of Constantinople. This effectively ended one of the world's great civilizations, the Byzantine Empire.

The Islamic world first learned of hand-held firearms

In the Middle Ages, soldiers used towers and cannons to attack the walls of a castle or buildings of a town.

from invading Mongols in the 13th century. Gunpowder weapons were not, however, easily accepted in the Middle East, where there was a long history of warriors' fighting from horseback with swords. People in the Middle East seemed uninterested in guns until the late 1400s. That was when Portuguese explorers used cannons and small firearms to destroy their armies, towns, and villages.

The first portable guns were nothing more than hand-held versions of cannons. The barrels even looked like the barrels of cannons. These weapons, invented around 1380, were called handgonnes. A handgonne consisted of a metal tube (a barrel) that was attached to the end of a wooden pole.

The shooter held the pole under his arm and used a glowing hot poker to light the gunpowder with his other hand.

Other than size, the difference between cannons and handgonnes was that cannons were fired at castle walls and forts, while handgonnes were fired at human beings. When Christopher Columbus reached the islands of the New World in

A medieval soldier holds an early hand-held firearm.

1492, an old handgonne was among the weapons his first landing party took ashore.

The awkward and limited handgonne was replaced by a gun that had a wooden stock. The stock supported the weapon against the body while the gun was being fired. This weapon was called a harquebus. In about 1410 the ignition system for guns was changed to a slow-burning fuse (or match) that was held in a metal clamp attached to the side of the gun. These were called matchlock guns.

The Japanese did not learn about guns from their neighbors, the Chinese. The first guns in Japan were matchlock weapons brought there in 1542 by three Portuguese sailors whose ship had been blown off course by a typhoon. The

The fuse of a matchlock gun from the early 1600s

The Story of Guns

southern Japanese island where the Portuguese sailors landed is called Tanegashima. Ever since then, that name has been the Japanese word for firearm. As late as the mid-1800s, long after matchlock guns had become obsolete in Western countries, they were the only kind of firearm in Japan.

All of the early personal firearms were relatively large weapons. Using them required a high degree of skill—especially loading them—and a lot of courage. They could blow up when firing, injuring or killing the shooter. Matchlocks were the guns carried by most early Americans. Pilgrims shot deer and other game with matchlocks. Colonists used them when fighting Native Americans.

Besides possibly being killed by the weapon being fired, using a burning match and fuse to fire a gun had other disadvantages. The enemy could see the glow of the burning match or smell it. The Dutch expression "to smell a match" means to sense danger. This expression originates from battles in which Spaniards used matchlock guns against the Dutch. Smelling the burning fuses of Spanish guns, Dutch soldiers watched for ambushes. Another disadvantage of matchlocks was that they were almost impossible to use in wet weather. Rain extinguished the matches required to light the fuses.

Italian artist and inventor Leonardo da Vinci designed a

An early 20th century illustration of a Pilgrim carrying a turkey he shot with his matchlock gun

better firearm in the 1490s. He drew charcoal sketches of a device that had a spring attached to the side of the firearm. When released, the spring drove a tooth-edged wheel against a piece of the mineral pyrite, causing sparks. The sparks ignited the gunpowder. The improved firing mechanism was called a wheel lock. It worked much the way a clock or wind-up toy works. A key was used to wind the spring, and the

Da Vinci's Guns

Leonardo da Vinci also designed machines with multiple cannons that could be fired either one after another or all together. Some people consider these the forerunner of the machine gun. Two of da Vinci's designs included racks with many guns. While the top row was being fired, the guns on the next rack could be loaded, and those on the third rack could be ready to load. Another design arranged the guns in a triangle, which would have better distributed the projectiles across a battlefield. Several of da Vinci's designs have been built in recent years by scholars and toy manufacturers and for study by the British military.

trigger released the wheel, creating the spark. With the wheel lock, the shooter could now simply aim the gun and fire it by pushing a lever, a form of trigger. Although almost all earlier improvements had been on large cannons, as soon as the wheel lock was invented, most technical refinements were to small arms: rifles and handguns.

Now not only could guns be carried cocked and ready to fire, but they could be fired with one hand. This was a requirement for soldiers who were riding horses. In addition guns were now more useful for hunting, because the animals being stalked were no longer alerted by the sight and smell of a burning match. One disadvantage of this design improvement was that, with no lighted fuse to signal that the gun was

A closeup of a 17th century English wheel lock mechanism shows the pyrite and wheel; below, a 16th century German wheel lock mechanism

ready to shoot, accidental firings became common. A byproduct was that the excuse "I didn't know the gun was loaded" was born. It became easier to harm another person and get away with it by pretending innocence. Another disadvantage was that wheel lock guns were more expensive to buy and maintain. Owners of these guns would now require the services of a watchmaker to maintain their firearms. As a result, wheel lock guns were owned almost exclusively by royalty.

Chapter **3**

Firearms of Early America

lthough the wheel lock was favored by royalty, the less expensive, less complicated matchlock was the gun that was used for the next 200 years by most of the world's armies. European and British military commanders of the 16th and 17th centuries did not want to replace the matchlocks they were using. They were happy that their soldiers' guns were simple to fire and to maintain.

Around 1600 the development of the flintlock—a device that produced the spark for igniting gunpowder by striking a chunk of flint against a piece of steel—revolutionized the world of firearms. The flintlock gun was faster and more reliable than the matchlock yet simpler and cheaper than the wheel lock. Invented in France, the flintlock eventually became the dominant firearm for civilians and military people in the New World and in Europe. The flintlock mechanism was applied to all sorts of guns, from muskets to rifles to revolvers.

For families settling in the American colonies and later

throughout the expanding United States, flintlock guns were essential tools. They were used to get meat for dinner and for killing predators. Many settlers had flintlock guns as protection against intruders. Almost all men and women in America knew how to handle muskets, and later rifles and shotguns. Fathers and mothers taught their children from an early age how to use guns. Parents and children shot and killed turkeys, ducks, geese, pigeons, rabbits, squirrels, coyotes, wolves, deer, elk, moose, bear, and bison. Animal fur and skins were used to make shoes, clothing,

The firing mechanism of a flintlock gun

Early settlers in the American colonies used flintlock guns to hunt game and to defend themselves against intruders.

and bedding. Killing an elk or bison was like going to a large store where you buy all your food and clothing: It was one-stop shopping.

The flintlock gun soon replaced the matchlock as the primary firearm of the world's militaries. In all the major, world-shaping wars of the 18th century, including the American Revolutionary War, flintlock guns played a decisive role.

In the 1700s, handguns and long guns were both used in combat, but they were not nearly as effective as modern versions. Sometimes the metal balls fired from guns wounded or killed the enemy. Often they did not. Long lines of soldiers on both sides of a battle stood and fired at the enemy. Then, because so few people would be killed or wounded, the soldiers had to rush toward the enemy. That's when the greatest killing started—not with shots fired, but with the bayonets attached to long guns. Benjamin Franklin considered guns so ineffective that at the start of the Revolutionary War in 1775, he suggested to the Continental Congress that the colonists arm themselves not with firearms but with bows and arrows.

Soldiers during the American Revolutionary War used flintlock guns with bayonets on the end so they could fight the enemy at close range as well as at a distance.

The Story of Guns

Despite their limitations, guns played a dominant role in the American Revolutionary War. Both the British and the Americans used flintlock muskets in all major battles. They were easy to load, and the large balls they fired had a fair amount of stopping power, which helped to break up attacks. The muskets were far from accurate, but since the enemy was standing shoulder to shoulder, simply aiming a lot of shots in their general direction meant you were likely to hit somebody. (The same principle applies to today's automatic

Soldiers in the American Revolutionary War stood shoulder to shoulder, firing on their enemy with flintlock guns.

weapons. They can create a wide field of fire, making it difficult for the enemy to avoid being struck.) If nothing else, the noise and smoke the muskets made caused panic and confusion.

When soldiers, such as snipers, needed greater accuracy, rifles were used. A rifled gun, unlike a "smoothbore," has spiraling grooves called rifles inside its barrel. Rifling causes the projectile—whether a lead ball or today's elongated bullet—to spin as it leaves the barrel. This makes it travel more accurately and penetrate what it strikes more deeply. The American long rifle, a descendant of the German jäger rifle that was brought to Pennsylvania by German and Swiss immigrants, was famed for its accuracy. It could hit a target at an unheard-of distance of 400 yards (366 meters)—the

Rifles used in the Revolutionary War

American frontiersman Daniel Boone carried a Kentucky-style American long rifle with him on his expeditions.

length of nearly four U.S. football fields. Long after the colonists had won their independence, the American long rifle remained the most popular gun on the American frontier.

As guns improved, they became more effective weapons of war. Elongated bullets replaced lead balls. Smokeless gun cotton took the place of gunpowder. The revolver, which fired six shots without having to be reloaded, eventually replaced the single-shot handgun. The repeating rifle, which can be fired more than once between loadings, replaced the single-shot Kentucky rifle—especially after ways were found to make rifles more accurate at ever-increasing distances.

Chapter 4

Weapons of the Wild West

Old movies and TV programs about the American West feature six-shooter showdowns on the Main Streets of frontier towns. But the reality of the Old West was less dramatic, less violent, and less decisive. Six-shooter or six-gun was a nickname for a Colt revolver, which had a cylinder that held six shots. The efficiency of the revolver, often called the Peacemaker, has been wildly exaggerated in Hollywood westerns, in which actors fire at one another from huge distances, rarely needing to reload.

Gunfights in the Old West occasionally took place, but they were almost never quick-draw face-offs in which the winner was the one who could get his gun out of its holster the fastest and shoot the other man dead. Most men in the American West did not carry handguns because their limited accuracy made them impractical weapons.

Rifles and shotguns were used to kill animals for food and to keep coyotes, wolves, and mountain lions away from livestock. Lawmen and hunters used rifles as their primary

Shootouts with handguns were rare in the Old West. Most men did not carry handguns and preferred to use rifles instead.

weapons because they were far more accurate than handguns. The double-barreled shotgun, which sprayed shot from its muzzle, was carried by many peace officers in the West, including Wyatt Earp and Bat Masterson. Men on the other side of the law had success with this gun, too. The notorious highwayman Black Bart (Charles E. Boles) used a double-barreled shotgun in all of his stagecoach robberies.

Lawmen, however, also carried handguns, because they sometimes needed a weapon that would be handy in close quarters. But when outlaws, who were often teenagers, tried to use handguns, the weapons often proved to be the cause of their demise.

Jesse James, one of the most famous American outlaws, gained a reputation of being a crack shot with a handgun when he was a Confederate guerrilla during the Civil War. The truth is that neither the weapon nor James was very capable. During the war, James shot off the tip of his finger while cleaning his revolver. Years later, during one of his infamous robberies, when he tried to kill an unarmed bank teller

A young Jesse James posed with his revolver.

who was crouched less than 10 feet (3 meters) away, he fired all six bullets his weapon held—and missed with every shot.

Cowboys who worked on ranches and took cattle to market carried handguns for killing snakes, destroying injured livestock, and turning aside cattle stampedes. Wild Bill Hickok, a notoriously vicious lawman of the Old West, used his six-shooters to kill stray dogs. The towns where Hickok worked paid him 25 cents for every dog he killed.

Cowboys on the open range regularly used handguns as hammers. They did not, however, use them for self-defense against cattle rustlers and outlaws. Handguns were not accurate or reliable enough for that.

Another reason that settlers in the West seldom used handguns for personal protection is that sidearms were

Percussion Firearms

The introduction of percussion ignition in about 1814 revolutionized firearm technology and laid the basis for the modern firearm. In this ignition system, a hammer strikes chemicals called priming compounds, causing them to explode. This in turn ignites a powder charge, causing the weapon to fire. Percussion arms were a huge improvement over flintlock guns. They were less prone to misfiring, virtually waterproof, and much simpler to load and fire. Literally millions of firearms, from the Hawken rifle used during the westward expansion to the handguns of Colt and Remington, were designed and built as percussion firearms. The current use of a brass cartridge to contain priming compound, powder charge, and projectile is simply the next logical step in standardizing and waterproofing the combined group further.

extremely expensive. When it was introduced in 1836, the Colt Paterson sold for $35. The average daily wage at the time was less than $1. The high price limited sales so much that the original Colt factory closed six years after it opened. It reopened in 1847 and went on to produce the Colt Peacemaker in 1873. This revolver was one of the most commonly carried firearms in the American West during the end of the 19th century.

When dealing with rustlers, wolves, coyotes, mountain lions, or bears, cowboys used the Winchester repeating rifle, which was introduced in 1866. The Winchester's lever action allowed for rapid repeat fire, and its long barrel helped make it unusually accurate. The Winchester was also used for hunting. Although it was designed for use on ranches and the

The Colt Peacemaker was also known as the Single Action Army Revolver, as well as a Colt .45. The number .45 refers to the internal diameter of the gun barrel.

The Story of Guns

open range, it soon became popular with soldiers.

The Winchester was not the world's first repeating rifle to see widespread use, however. The first was the Spencer, which was made in 1860 by Christopher Spencer, a Union loyalist in Connecticut. Spencer also invented one of the world's first automobiles, a steam-powered vehicle he drove to and from his workshop—until police officers in his town asked him to stop because his car scared the horses.

President Abraham Lincoln ordered the Spencer repeating rifle for Union cavalry soldiers in the Civil War. Spencer rifles could shoot 14 rounds a minute. They were dramatically superior weapons compared with the muskets used by Confederate troops. The Civil War also gave rise to the United States Sharpshooters, a highly trained group of snipers for the Union Army who used Spencer rifles for very important targets. No longer could a Confederate military commander or government official relax in the open, seemingly out of rifle range. If a person could be seen, he could be hit. Union snipers added a new dimension to warfare, one that remains influential today.

In addition to rifles, Union and Confederate soldiers carried handguns. Particularly popular were Colt and Remington revolvers. A small, easily concealed handgun called a derringer pistol played an especially unfortunate role in the war. John Wilkes Booth, a bitter and deranged Confederate sympathizer, used a derringer to kill President Lincoln. Derringer pistols, popular in the mid-1800s, figured in so many murders that the guns themselves became famous. Almost everyone in America and in Europe knew about derringers from having read newspaper stories about the many crimes associated with them.

The American Civil War did more to increase the spread and killing efficiency of guns than any other war in history. The weapons of the Civil War were so successful that, during the four years the war lasted, in a nation of fewer than 32 million people, more than 620,000 people died. Thus the Civil War started the age of industrialized warfare.

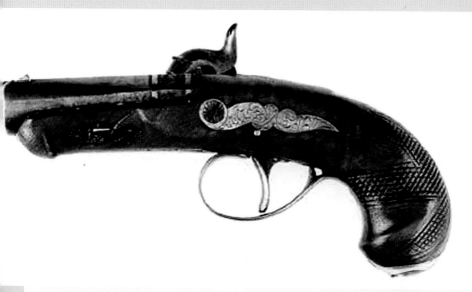

The derringer that John Wilkes Booth used to assassinate President Lincoln in 1865 was found at the scene of the crime—the presidential box at Ford's Theatre in Washington, D.C.

Chapter 5

Guns Go Automatic

During the Civil War, North Carolina physician Richard Gatling was horrified by the number of young men whose lives were being lost not to enemy bullets but to disease. He wrote later: "It occurred to me that if I could invent a machine—a gun—which could by its rapidity of fire, enable one man to do as much battle duty as a hundred, that it would supercede the necessity of large armies, and consequently, exposure to battle and disease [would] be greatly diminished."

Gatling patented his design for the Gatling gun in 1862. It was a large, six-barreled weapon that was operated by turning a crank on the side of the gun. The Gatling gun was mounted on a flat surface such as platform or the back of a wagon, and it fired a phenomenal 200 rounds per minute. The Gatling gun was used by Union forces late in the war and had a devastating impact on the enemy. As a result, the U.S. Army ordered 100 of these new guns, and soon armies around the world were buying them.

SCIENTIFIC AMERICAN

A WEEKLY JOURNAL OF PRACTICAL INFORMATION, ART, SCIENCE, MECHANICS, CHEMISTRY, AND MANUFACTURES.

Vol. XL.—No. 24.
[NEW SERIES.]

NEW YORK, JUNE 14, 1879.

[$3.20 per Annum.
[POSTAGE PREPAID.]

The June 14, 1879, issue of *Scientific American* featured the Gatling gun on its cover.

After the Civil War, the Gatling gun was mainly used to expand European and American empires by killing warriors of societies that did not have such lethal machines. The

The Story of Guns

The Puckle Gun

Nearly everyone believes that the Gatling gun was the first rapid-fire gun. But the credit belongs to James Puckle, an English inventor, lawyer, and writer who invented the Defence Gun, better known as the Puckle gun. He demonstrated his gun for the British military in 1718. It was a tripod-mounted flintlock weapon with a multishot revolving cylinder. Puckle designed the gun to prevent enemies from boarding English ships. It could fire nine shots per minute at a time when the standard musket could be loaded and fired only once or twice per minute. There were two versions of the gun. One was intended for use against Christian enemies. It fired round bullets. The second Puckle gun, for use against Muslim Turks, fired square bullets. Those, Puckle said, were more damaging and would convince the Turks of the "benefits of Christian civilization." The Puckle gun was never mass-produced, mostly because British gunsmiths at the time couldn't make the many complicated parts.

An 1890 illustration of a sailor firing a Gatling gun

English used it to nearly eliminate entire tribes in Africa and the Middle East. Russia destroyed Turkish cavalry units and nomads of central Asia. The United States used Gatling guns in the Spanish-American War (1898) and the Philippine-American War (1899–1902). The U.S. cavalry used Gatling guns against villages of Plains Indians in the late 1800s.

In 1881 Hiram Maxim, an American inventor, visited the Paris Electrical Exhibition. He had already invented a mousetrap and the world's first automatic fire sprinkler, but an American at the exhibition told him, "If you want to make a lot of money, invent something that will enable these

The Story of Guns

Europeans to cut each other's throats with greater facility."

Maxim moved to London, became a British citizen, and began trying to create an effective machine gun. In 1885 he demonstrated the world's first portable, fully automatic machine gun to the British army. An automatic gun cocks, reloads, and fires as long as the trigger is depressed. The Maxim gun could fire at the amazing rate of 600 to 700

Hiram Maxim demonstrated his Maxim gun to a young boy in 1880s Great Britain.

rounds a minute. It used its recoil to rapidly eject a spent cartridge and load a new one. Ammunition was fed to it on a belt. The gun could fire without stopping until the entire belt of bullets was used up.

The British army adopted Maxim's machine gun in 1889. It was first used in Africa in 1893 during the First Matabele War. Fifty British soldiers fought off 5,000 Matabele warriors with just four Maxim guns. Maxim sold the rights to his machine gun to armies around the world. He became enormously rich and was knighted by England's Queen Victoria for having made the most efficient killing weapon the world had yet known.

British soldiers fired a Maxim gun as part of training exercises in 1915.

The Story of Guns

Chapter 6

Weapons of War

D uring the 20th century, guns and other weapons were developed to the point that they became immeasurably more lethal than they had been the century before. The century also marked the first time that wars became so large that they involved nearly every nation in the world.

Throughout the century, killing became more and more

A World War I poster brought out "the big guns" to encourage enlistment.

mechanized and easier to accomplish. More people were killed in the wars of the 20th century than in all previous military conflicts combined. This happened chiefly because guns had become so lethally efficient.

World War I began in 1914. Much of the war was fought by soldiers in deep trenches. Nearly a million soldiers died, not only because of wounds caused by guns, but also from infections and diseases worsened by filthy battlefield conditions. Hiram Maxim's machine gun prolonged the war by proving itself to be the ideal weapon to defend trenches. Its tremendous rate of fire and range could kill anything that was caught on open ground. So soldiers on both sides stayed far down in the trenches for as long as they could.

Soldiers in trenches fired at the opposing side across an empty area known as no man's land.

The World's Biggest Guns

All of the biggest guns that have ever been built were made during the 20th century. The biggest of these are cannons. They are, in fact, the only weapons that military people call guns. They call rifles and handguns small arms. About three-fourths of casualties during World War I resulted from the use of cannons.

The Paris gun was a World War I German cannon that fired shells up to 80 miles (129 kilometers). The gun weighed 256 tons (232 metric tons) and was mounted on a concrete carriage with a turntable. Its barrel was 92 feet (28 m) long, with a 20-foot (6-m) extension. It was called the Paris gun because the German military used it to bombard the city of Paris. It was not very accurate and was used mostly to awe and frighten the enemy.

The biggest gun ever used in a war is the Gustav gun, which was built for Adolf Hitler in 1941. It weighed a massive 1,344 tons (1,219 metric tons) and required a 500-man crew to operate it. The Gustav gun was so huge it was carried by train on specially built twin railroad tracks. The Gustav gun shot 16,540-pound (7,502-kilogram) concrete-piercing shells and could strike targets 29 miles (47 km) away.

Near the end of the war, generals wanted a machine gun that had the firepower of the Maxim gun but was smaller and could be used by one man. With his invention of the hand-held Thompson submachine gun, American General John T. Thompson aimed to satisfy this need and thus end the war. But the first shipment of guns intended for the battlefields of Europe arrived at the docks in New York City on November 11, 1918, the day the war ended.

After World War I, General Thompson's submachine gun became the favored weapon of American gangsters, who nicknamed it the Tommy gun. On Valentine's Day 1929, gangster kingpin Al Capone sent hired killers, including two men dressed as police officers, to kill rival gang members in a car garage in Chicago. Seven men were lined up against a brick wall of the garage and were shot with

Soldiers practiced "dry firing" the Thompson submachine gun before firing with live ammunition.

hundreds of machine-gun rounds. Called the St. Valentine's Day Massacre, it was the most spectacular murder in gang history, and it made Capone famous. The murder weapons were two Tommy guns.

No one was ever arrested for the murders, but newspaper coverage led to a public outcry against machine guns. The National Firearms Act of 1934 made it illegal for citizens to own fully automatic weapons. Since then automatic weapons have been strictly regulated by the U.S. Justice Department's Bureau of Alcohol, Tobacco, Firearms, and Explosives.

The St. Valentine's Day Massacre was reported on the front page of *The Chicago Daily News*.

Regulating Firearms

The Bureau of Alcohol, Tobacco, Firearms, and Explosives is responsible for regulating the firearms and explosives industry in the United States. Known as ATF, the bureau issues federal firearms licenses to sellers and inspects their places of business. It is also involved in programs aimed at reducing gun violence by targeting and arresting violent offenders who illegally possess firearms. ATF special agents are in charge of investigating any federal crime committed with a firearm or explosive.

The next major refinement in automatic weapons came in 1944, toward the end of World War II. It was the assault rifle, which combined the most lethally efficient features of the rifle, the submachine gun, and the carbine. Assault rifles use controllable bursts of fire at short range like submachine guns but have riflelike accuracy at medium ranges. They can be used for single shots, fully automatic bursts, or sustained automatic fire.

The first assault rifle was the German military's extremely deadly MP44. Adolf Hitler called the MP44 the *sturmgewehr* ("storm rifle"). By the end of the war, Soviet engineer Mikhail Kalashnikov had adapted the German design to create the AK-47. Officially introduced in 1947, the AK-47—also known as the Kalashnikov—eventually became the world's most widely used assault weapon.

In 1964 the United States military services began using their own assault rifle, the M-16, which became standard issue for U.S. soldiers in the Vietnam War. Variations on the M-16 design were adopted in the 1980s by the 15 member

Mikhail Kalashnikov posed with his invention, the AK-47.

countries of the North Atlantic Treaty Organization. Today the M-16 is the firearm most often used by military forces around the world.

The M-16 is both an automatic and semiautomatic weapon. Unlike a purely automatic weapon, which keeps cocking, firing, and reloading as long as the trigger is pressed, a semiautomatic weapon cocks, fires only one round, and reloads when the trigger is squeezed. Like many modern military guns, the M-16 has a switch that lets it be fired in either a semiautomatic or fully automatic mode. Modern assault weapons can shoot up to 700 rounds per minute.

A Vietnam War-era soldier carried an M-16 equipped with a scope designed for night vision.

Chapter 7

The Spread of Arms

After World War II, many people hoped there would be a long period of peace. What happened instead is that people with different ideas about the best form of government began to compete against each other in what was called the Cold War. On one side were the Soviet Union, the People's Republic of China, and many of the nations of Eastern Europe. This group was often called the communists. The opposing side consisted of the United States, Britain, and the nations of Western Europe. These countries were usually referred to as the democracies, the free nations, or the Free World. For more than 40 years after World War II, both sides spent trillions of dollars making and storing millions of new, ever-more-lethal guns.

Both sides in the Cold War tried to recruit allies in the rest of the world while stopping the opposing side from making allies. One way they tried to do this was by selling guns to almost any government or revolutionary group that they thought could be persuaded to join them. In the 1950s in the

United States, the domino theory became popular among some politicians and military leaders. The domino theory was the idea that if a noncommunist country became communist, that could make all the countries around it become communist. The countries would fall like dominoes. Soon, according to this theory, communists would take over the world. This led the U.S. government to sell or give millions of its guns to almost any group of people in any country who said their goal was to crush a communist or socialist group in their country.

The United States, the Soviet Union, and China all sold

The United States sent arms to Afghan resistance groups that were fighting the communist Soviet Union, which invaded Afghanistan in 1979.

The Story of Guns

huge numbers of guns to governments and rebel groups. Eventually Israel, Germany, Belgium, Italy, and Brazil did, too. This meant that huge quantities of weapons were sold or given to potentially dangerous people all over the world. Guns are very durable machines that last for a very long time. The guns that were sold by all these countries are out there in the world today and are regularly used to kill people on many continents.

The 1988 breakup of the Soviet Union flooded the international guns market with Soviet-made weapons. Guerrillas and paramilitary groups bought many of them. And many were bought by powerful international drug dealers, such as the cocaine cartels in Colombia and Mexico and the heroin cartels in Afghanistan. Today the Soviet-made AK-47 is the gun most often used by terrorists and other criminals worldwide.

Particularly troubling is what has happened in Africa. Millions of assault rifles, which are lightweight, highly portable, and devastatingly lethal in the hands of even young or poorly trained users, were shipped to Africa during the Cold War. After the collapse of the Soviet Union, former Soviet weapons manufacturers sold as many guns as they could in Africa at very low prices. Decades later these guns are in the hands of outlaws. In some parts of Africa, an AK-47 can be bought for $6 or traded for a chicken or a sack of grain.

A Liberian child soldier posed with his AK-47 before surrendering it in a U.N. arms-reduction program.

The international sale of guns is a massive business. And it is a massive problem for peacekeeping agencies such as the United Nations. A 2009 U.N. survey found that the United States alone was responsible for about half of the legal international gun sales between 2000 and 2006. No other country sold more than 4 percent of the global total.

Various international organizations, including the U.N., and domestic groups, such as the Small Arms Working Group in the United States, have committed themselves to

Child Soldiers

More than 120,000 children in Africa, some as young as 7 years old, are being used as soldiers. The children are kidnapped from their schools and homes, even from their beds. Often they are forced to watch their parents being slaughtered. Then they are brainwashed, trained to use guns, given drugs, and sent into battle with orders to kill. Sometimes their assault rifles are taller than they are. Martin, a 12-year-old boy from Uganda, told the organization Human Rights Watch: "Early on when my brothers and I were captured, the LRA [Lord's Resistance Army] explained to us that all five brothers couldn't serve in the LRA because we would not perform well. So they tied up my two younger brothers and invited us to watch. Then they beat them with sticks until two of them died. They told us it would give us strength to fight. My youngest brother was 9 years old."

In 2002 the International Criminal Court made it a war crime to use children under 15 as soldiers. Yet according to the United Nations, child soldiers have been widely used in the last decade in more than 30 countries. Today there may be as many as 300,000 child soldiers in the world.

limiting the trade in, and spread of, guns around the world. More than 500,000 people are killed each year by the use of small arms, and there are more than 600 million such guns in the world.

More than 1,000 companies in almost 100 countries are involved some way in making small arms. With the United States and the Soviet Union both having given and sold millions and millions of guns to people all around the globe, we now live in a world that is neck-deep in firearms.

Parts of the Beretta 925 semiautomatic pistol await assembly and final touches at the Beretta factory in Italy.

The Story of Guns

Chapter 8

A World Transformed by Violence

olitical assassinations have been taking place for thousands of years. As the use of guns became more widespread, however, so did assassinations. World War I was started by a political assassination when, on June 28, 1914, Archduke Franz Ferdinand of Austria-Hungary was shot and killed by an assassin with a handgun. Other assassinations have changed the direction of nations and halted political and social reform movements. With the spread of the gun, formerly powerless peasants could become powerful in a moment, simply by pulling a trigger.

Four U.S. presidents have been assassinated. Abraham Lincoln, James Garfield, William McKinley, and John F. Kennedy were all killed with guns. There have been unsuccessful gun assassination attempts on several other presidents. Gun assassinations have killed some of the most influential people in the world, including nonviolent political activists Mohandas Gandhi and Martin Luther King Jr.

Political and social leaders are, of course, not the only

Civil rights leader Andrew Young (left) and others pointed in the direction of the shooter after the April 4, 1968, assassination of Martin Luther King Jr., who lay at their feet.

people who have been killed in peacetime by guns. Between 1979 and 2009, gun violence killed more than 120,000 children and teenagers in America. Every year since the 1970s, more children and teenagers have died from gun violence than from cancer, pneumonia, flu, asthma, AIDS, and all other natural causes combined.

The United States has the least restrictive gun control laws in the developed world. What are the results of having the weakest gun controls of any developed nation? The rate of firearm deaths among kids under age 15 is 12 times as high in the United States as in the other 24 largest developed countries combined. American kids are 16 times as likely to be murdered with a gun, 11 times as likely to commit suicide

A student in Chicago, Illinois, protested handgun use during a public rally against gun violence.

with a gun, and nine times as likely to die from a firearm accident as are children in the other 24 largest industrialized countries combined. Every hour two American kids are killed by people using guns. Every day nearly 100 Americans die from gun violence. Nearly 13,000 people are murdered with guns every year in the United States.

From its beginnings, the United States has had an intimate relationship with guns. Firearms are the only kind of personal property that the U.S. Constitution says cannot be regulated by the government. Many people argue that increasing gun control goes against the wishes of the country's founding fathers. They further argue that gun control

Many Americans argue that gun control limits individual rights and makes people less safe.

makes average citizens less safe by restricting their ability to defend themselves with firearms.

Still, owning and using a gun carries great responsibility. Many people in the United States are working to make guns safer. A recent positive development in gun technology is the "smart gun," which has computerized sensors built into the handle. The sensors capture the unique pattern and pressure of the gun owner's grip, plus the size, shape, and weight of

Recent School Shootings

May 21, 1998: *Springfield, Oregon* Two students were shot to death and 22 were wounded in the cafeteria at Thurston High School by 15-year-old Kip Kinkel. He had been arrested a day earlier for bringing a gun to school, and released. His parents were later found shot to death at home.

April 20, 1999: *Littleton, Colorado* Fourteen students (including the killers) and one teacher were killed and 23 others were wounded at Columbine High School in the nation's deadliest high school shooting. Eric Harris, 18, and Dylan Klebold, 17, had plotted for a year to kill at least 500 people and blow up their school. At the end of their hourlong rampage, they turned their guns on themselves.

February 29, 2000: *Mount Morris Township, Michigan* Six-year-old Kayla Rolland was shot dead at Buell Elementary School. The assailant was identified as a 6-year-old boy with a .32-caliber handgun.

October 3, 2006: *Nickel Mines, Pennsylvania* Thirty-two-year-old Carl Charles Roberts IV entered the one-room West Nickel Mines Amish School and shot 10 schoolgirls, ranging in age from 6 to 13 years old, and then himself. Five of the girls and Roberts died.

April 16, 2007: *Blacksburg, Virginia* A 23-year-old student at Virginia Tech, Cho Seung-Hui, shot and killed two students in a dorm, and then killed 30 more two hours later in a classroom building. His suicide brought the death toll to 33, making the shooting rampage the most deadly in U.S. history. Fifteen others were wounded.

May 5, 2009: *Canandaigua, New York* A 17-year-old male high school student committed suicide, shooting himself with a modified shotgun in a men's restroom in the athletic wing of the school. He had 30 rounds of ammunition in his pockets and locker.

Inventor Michael Recce demonstrated an early model of his "smart gun" with grip recognition technology.

the owner's hand. If a person other than the owner tries to shoot the gun, the sensor reading will not match the stored information about the owner, and the gun will not fire. The smart gun's grip recognition system makes it impossible for another adult or—more important—a child to use the gun. Gun-safety advocates applaud such efforts while recognizing that much more needs to be done.

As we study the history of guns, we see that people have always used weapons to defend their interests and themselves. Guns continue to evolve as our use of them does. Guns have truly changed the world.

Timeline

142 Taoist monk Wei Boyang writes about gunpowder, describing it as three mineral powders that, when mixed, "fly and dance"

700s Chinese inventors make weapons using gunpowder, including flamethrowers, bombs, and mines

1268–1273 Kublai Khan uses cannons in the siege of Siang Yang

1380 The first portable firearm, called the handgonne, is invented

1411 Matchlock guns are introduced

1453 Turkish invaders use cannons to knock down the walls of Constantinople

1500s Wheel lock guns are invented

1600s Flintlock guns are invented

1718 James Puckle demonstrates his Defence Gun—better known as the Puckle gun—for the British military

c. 1814 Percussion firearms are introduced

1860 Christopher Spencer invents the repeating rifle

1862 Richard Gatling patents his design for the Gatling gun

1866 The Winchester repeating rifle is introduced

1885 Inventor Hiram Maxim demonstrates the Maxim gun, the world's first portable automatic machine gun, to the British army

June 28, 1914 Gavrilo Princip assassinates Austria-Hungary's Archduke Franz Ferdinand with a handgun, leading to World War I

November 11, 1918 World War I ends; Thompson submachine guns arrive at New York City too late to ship to battlefields in Europe

February 14, 1929 Thompson submachine guns are used to kill seven Chicago gang members in the St. Valentine's Day Massacre

1941 The Gustav Gun, the largest gun ever used in a war, is built for German leader Adolf Hitler

1944 Assault rifles are introduced with the German military's MP44

1947 The AK-47, designed by Soviet engineer Mikhail Kalashnikov, is introduced; it eventually becomes the world's most widely used assault weapon

1964 The U.S. military begins using an American-made assault rifle, the M-16, in the Vietnam War

1988 The breakup of the Soviet Union floods the international guns market with Soviet-made weapons

April 16, 2007 Thirty-three students are killed and 15 are wounded at Virginia Tech in the deadliest school shooting in U.S. history

2009 A bill is introduced in Congress that provides criminal penalties for improper licensing and registration of firearms

Glossary

bayonet	blade attached to the end of a rifle and used as a weapon in close combat
carbine	short-barreled rifle or musket
cavalry	soldiers mounted on horseback
cylinder	container that holds a powder charge, a projectile, and a primer for use in a firearm
guerrilla	soldier who is not part of a country's regular army and who fights in groups that use small, surprise attacks
machine gun	automatic firearm capable of sustained fire
matchlock	early form of gun that used a smoldering match held in an armlike device; pulling the trigger released the arm and dropped the match onto the powder
musket	gun with a long barrel used before rifles were invented
muzzle	open front end of the barrel
recoil	rearward movement of the barrel or weapon in reaction to the forward movement of the bullet
revolvers	weapons whose ammunition is held in a rotating cylinder
shotguns	smoothbore firearms that usually fire small metal pellets, called shot, rather than single projectiles
shrapnel	fragments thrown through the air by the force of an explosion
skirmish	small battle
submachine gun	portable firearm capable of the fully automatic fire of a machine gun but that uses pistol ammunition

Additional Resources

Investigate Further

Bark, Jaspre. *Journal of Inventions: Leonardo da Vinci*. Berkeley, Calif.: Silver Dolphin Books, 2009.

Beah, Ishmael. *A Long Way Gone: Memoirs of a Boy Soldier*. New York: Farrar, Straus and Giroux, 2007.

Miller, Debra A., ed. *Guns and Violence*. Detroit: Greenhaven Press, 2009.

Richie, Jason. *Weapons: Designing the Tools of War*. Minneapolis: Oliver Press, 2000.

Souter, Gerry. *Military Rifles: Fierce Firepower*. Berkeley Heights, N.J.: Enslow Publishers, 2006.

Wyckoff, Edwin Brit. *The Man Behind the Gun: Samuel Colt and His Revolver*. Berkeley Heights, N.J.: Enslow Publishers, 2010.

Internet Sites

FactHound offers a safe, fun way to find Internet sites related to this book. All of the sites on FactHound have been researched by our staff.

Here's all you do:

Visit *www.facthound.com*

FactHound will fetch the best sites for you!

Select Bibliography

Chase, Kenneth. *Firearms: A Global History to 1700*. Cambridge, U.K.: Cambridge University Press, 2003.

Diagram Group. *The New Weapons of the World Encyclopedia: An International Encyclopedia From 5000 B.C. to the 21st Century*. New York: St. Martin's Griffin, 2007.

Gun: A Visual History. New York: DK Publishing, 2007.

Herring, Hal. *Famous Firearms of the Old West: From Wild Bill Hickok's Colt Revolvers to Geronimo's Winchester: Twelve Guns That Shaped Our History*. Guilford, Conn.: TwoDot, 2008.

Keegan, John. *The Face of Battle*. New York: Penguin Books, 1976.

Kennedy, David. *Guns of the Wild West*. Philadelphia: Courage Books, 2005.

Peterson, Harold L. *Pageant of the Gun: A Treasury of Stories of Firearms: Their Romance and Lore, Development, and Use Through Ten Centuries*. Garden City, N.Y.: Doubleday, 1967.

Spencer, Michael. *Early Firearms, 1300–1800*. New York: Shire Publications, 2008.

Walter, John. *The Guns That Won the West: Firearms on the American Frontier, 1848–1898*. St. Paul, Minn.: MBI Pub., 2006.

About the Author

Katherine McLean Brevard is the author of several fiction and nonfiction books for young people. She enjoys reading and writing about American and world history, the natural world, nutrition, and preventive medicine. She lives on a farm in the mountains of North Carolina with her husband, Davis, and their dogs, Charlie and Chester.

Index

Index